O9-AIG-919

One Day Fun Days

A Collection of Mini Themes for Any Day of the Year

Edited by:
Ada Goren
Angie Kutzer

Written by:
LeeAnn Collins, Susan DeRiso, Rhonda Dominguez,
Kristin Ganoung, Ada Goren, Kathy H. Lee, Nancy M. Lotzer,
Michele Menzel, Katie Padilla, Chrissy Yuhouse

Illustrated by:
Cathy Spangler Bruce, Pam Crane, Clevell Harris, Susan Hodnett,
Sheila Krill, Theresa Lewis, Kimberly Richard, Greg D. Rieves,
Rebecca Saunders

Cover designed by:
Cathy Spangler Bruce, Nick Greenwood, Kimberly Richard

www.themailbox.com

Manufactured in the United States

10 9 8 7 6 5 4 3 2 1

TABLE OF CONTENTS

"What in the world is a one day fun day?"

- It's a day full of songs, stories, snacks, centers, and other super stuff!
- It's a break from your regular routine.
- It's a topic that's just a *little* out of the ordinary.
- It's a whole day of creative learning activities.
- It's a mini unit with maximum appeal.
- It's a theme all by itself or a way to extend a longer, related theme.

It's all this and more! Just turn the page to find **20** fabulous one day fun days, planned and ready for you to use!

Banana Day

Little ones are sure to go bananas over these "a-peel-ing" ideas!

ideas contributed by Nancy M. Lotzer

Circle Time:
Hey, Mr. Tally Man, Tally Me Bananas!

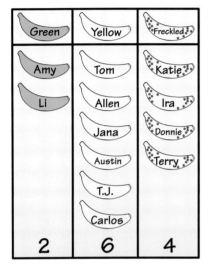

Green	Yellow	Freckled
Amy	Tom	Katie
Li	Allen	Ira
	Jana	Donnie
	Austin	Terry
	T.J.	
	Carlos	
2	**6**	**4**

Start your Banana Day with this tasty tally! In advance, purchase three bananas—one green, one yellow, and one freckled (yellow with brown specks). Also use the banana pattern on page 6 to make a class supply plus one extra of the following banana types: green, yellow, and freckled. Prepare a simple graph on a sheet of poster board as shown, using the extra banana cutouts to label the columns.

Gather your little ones and explain to them that as a banana changes color, its flavor and texture also change. Green bananas are firm and tart. Yellow bananas are softer and sweeter. Freckled bananas are very soft and have the sweetest taste. Next, peel and cut each banana into tidbits for youngsters to try. Have them taste the green banana first, then the yellow banana, and finally the freckled banana. Talk about the differences in flavor and texture. After youngsters have tried all three bananas, have each child choose a banana cutout to represent the type she liked best. Write her name on her banana and attach it to the graph. When all the votes are in, count the bananas in each column and write the tally at the bottom. Which colors were most and least favored? Save the leftover banana cutouts to use with "Banana Split Party" on page 5.

Rhythm-and-Rhyme Time:
Say It and Sign It

Teach your banana fans this poem and the accompanying sign-language signs.

Bananas are a yellow fruit
I like to munch each day.
Mom puts one in my lunchbox
When I go to school to play.

banana   yellow   put   box

I   munch   I   school

Transition Time:
Go Bananas!

Touch the banana to your foot, then hop four times.

Got a minute? Get a banana—and try this fun activity that emphasizes auditory memory and movement skills. To prepare, purchase a plastic banana or make a banana cutout from yellow poster board. Then make a supply of yellow bananas using the pattern on page 6. Program each cutout with two- or three-part directions. Place the banana cutouts in a paper lunch bag. When you have a minute to fill, ask a child to reach into the bag and pull out a banana. Hand him the plastic banana and read aloud the directions on the cutout. Once he's successfully followed the directions, invite another child to go bananas!

Project Time:
Bunches of Bananas

We all know bananas make a handy snack, but this project proves they make a pretty handy art project, too! Set up your art center with white construction paper and two containers of paint—one yellow and one green. Scent the yellow paint with banana extract. To make a bunch of bananas, paint a child's eight fingers with the yellow paint. Then paint just the upper part of the child's palms with green paint. Have the child hold both hands close together and make a print on a sheet of white paper. When the paint is dry, cut around each banana bunch. Use the cutouts to decorate your classroom door, adding the title "We're Going Bananas Today!"

Movement Time:
Leaf Leapers

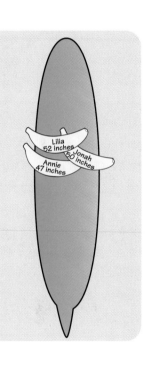

Leap into this activity that combines math and movement. To prepare, cut a six-foot leaf shape from green bulletin board paper or from four sheets of 12" x 18" green construction paper taped together. Attach the leaf to a wall with one end touching the floor. Also, make a class supply of the banana pattern on page 6 on yellow construction paper. Label each cutout with a child's name.

Begin the activity by telling students that the leaves of banana plants grow to more than six feet long! Show them the paper leaf and have a student stand next to it for comparison. Do any of the children think they can reach the top of the leaf? It's time to try! On each child's turn, hand her her banana cutout with a bit of Sticky-Tac or looped tape on the back. Encourage her to stand next to the leaf and jump as high as she can, sticking her banana cutout onto the leaf to mark the height of her leap. Help each child use a tape measure to measure her leap and record that information on her banana cutout. Encourage the children to compare their leaps, emphasizing words such as *high, higher,* and *highest.*

Date: Friday, May 21   Time: 11:00 A.M.

Please contact me if you can send any of these items.

Needed per person:
a small bowl
a plastic spoon
a plastic knife
half a banana
a scoop of ice cream
a cherry

Needed per class party:
tub(s) of whipped topping
bottle(s) of chocolate syrup
candy sprinkles or chopped nuts

You're Invited
to a
Banana Split Party!

Mrs. Lotzer's Class

Snacktime:
Banana Split Party

What better way to end Banana Day than with a banana split party? A few days in advance, program and copy the invitation on page 6 for each child's parents and/or school staff members you wish to invite. Use the leftover banana cutouts from the circle time activity on page 4 as nametags for your party. During the party, have adults help little ones assemble their banana splits. Before your guests leave, invite them to listen as your students perform the sign-language rhyme on page 4. Mmm...delicious fun!

Banana Pattern

Use with "Hey, Mr. Tally Man, Tally Me Bananas!" and "Go Bananas!" on page 4 and "Leaf Leapers" on page 5.

Invitation

Use with "Banana Split Party" on page 5.

Date: Time:

You're Invited
to a
Banana Split Party!

Dear Family:

On _____, we will be having Beach Ball
(date)

Day at school. We need a few beach balls for our activities.

Would you mind sending in an old beach ball you may

have at your house? The beach balls may get a little messy,

but we'll do our best to clean them before returning them

to you!

Thanks for your help!

Button
Use with "*Beach Ball* Starts With *B*" on page 8.

Black-and-White Day

You'll find the combination of black and white on lots of things, from artwork to zebras! Explore this fascinating color pair with a day full of activities, or incorporate a few of these ideas into a unit on colors.

ideas contributed by Rhonda Dominguez and Ada Goren

Rhythm-and-Rhyme Time:
Start the Day With a Poem

Welcome youngsters to Black-and-White Day by reciting this poem. Then head right into your circle-time activity.

"What's your favorite color?"
It's a question we often pose.
Answers might be "blue" or "pink"—
You know how it goes.
Black and white aren't thought of.
They're simply overlooked.
But let's explore this color pair
And soon you will be hooked!

Center Time:
Black-and-White Art

It's all here in black and white—all the materials to make a unique art project, that is! Set up your art center with plenty of art materials in black and white, such as paper, paint, yarn, glitter, pom-poms, and pipe cleaners. Encourage little ones to visit this center to create a one-of-a-kind black-and-white painting, collage, or sculpture.

Circle Time:
Dressed for the Day

Prior to Black-and-White Day, send each child home with a copy of the parent note on page 12. During circle time on Black-and-White Day, invite each child to stand and show what she is wearing in the colors for the day. Then help youngsters sort themselves by their clothing. You might make groups based on articles of clothing that are solid white or black, or articles that have black-and-white stripes, dots, or other designs. Don't forget to sort by black and white on shoes, socks, buttons, or even hair accessories!

Project Time:
Extra! Extra!

What's black and white and read all over? A newspaper, of course! And making a class newspaper is a perfect project for Black-and-White Day! To prepare, photocopy the newspaper format on page 12 for each child. Then cover a half sheet of tagboard with real newspaper for each child. Bring in a newspaper and discuss with your students what it is and how it is used. Explain that adults read a newspaper to find out about things and people in the world around them. Then give each child a copy of the newspaper format and have her write or dictate to fill in the blanks. Have her use a black crayon to add a drawing of herself or glue a photocopy of her school photo in the space provided. Have each child glue her completed sheet to her newspaper-covered tagboard. Bind the pages together behind a tagboard cover that reads "Extra! Extra! Read All About Us!" Invite little ones to take turns taking the class newspaper home to share with their families.

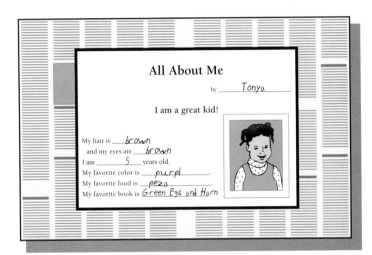

Transition Time:
Black-and-White Riddles

When you have a moment to spare on Black-and-White Day, get your students thinking with a black-and-white riddle. Just give them two or three clues about a black-and-white object or animal and challenge them to figure out the answer. Here are a few to get you started.

This is an animal.
It looks like a horse.
It has stripes.
(a zebra)

These are keys, but they don't open locks.
They make music.
(piano keys)

This is a bird, but it doesn't fly.
It lives where it is very cold.
(a penguin)

This is something good to eat.
It's frozen.
You might eat it in a cone.
(chocolate chip ice cream)

Snacktime:
Cookie Faces

It's hard to think of black and white without thinking of Oreo® cookies! Add a couple of other black-and-white ingredients, and you'll have this snack that's just right for Black-and-White Day. To make one Cookie Face, a child carefully twists open an Oreo cookie, trying to leave the cream filling intact on one side. He places two mini chocolate chip eyes atop the white filling and then creates a mouth from a short length of black string licorice. Serve the Cookie Face with a cup of cold, white milk. Yum!

Parent Note

Use with "Dressed for the Day" on page 10.

Dear Family:

On ______________________ (date), we'll be having Black-and-White Day at school. Please help your child pick out one or more articles of clothing in black, white, or a black-and-white combination to wear to school that day.

Thanks for your help!

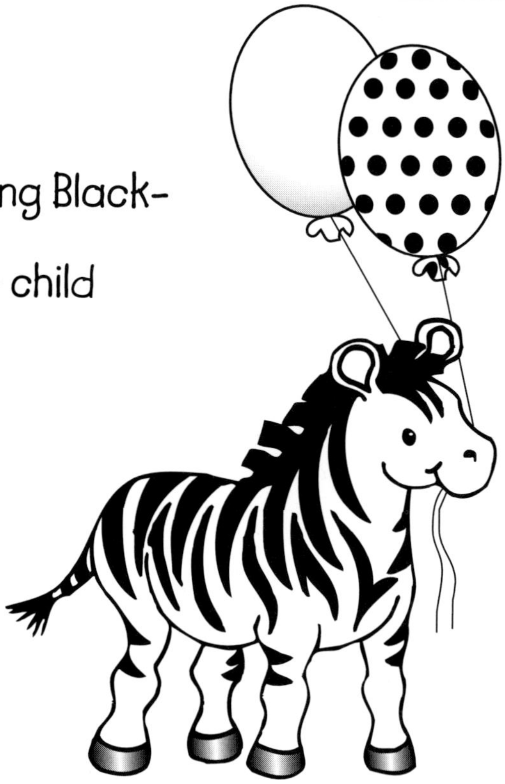

Newspaper Format

Use with "Extra! Extra!" on page 11.

All About Me

by ______________________

I am a great kid!

My hair is __________

and my eyes are __________.

I am ______________ years old.

My favorite color is ____________________.

My favorite food is ____________________.

My favorite book is ____________________.

Button Day

Spend a whole day with these "fasten-ating" little manipulatives! Or pick and choose from the activities in this unit to reinforce sorting and patterning skills or to add fun to a focus on the letter *B*.

ideas contributed by Kathleen Padilla

Storytime:
The Button Box

Share the very informative story *The Button Box* by Margarette S. Reid (Puffin Books). Afterward, invite little ones to have a "hole" lot of fun comparing some real buttons! To prepare, send home the note on page 15 asking parents to donate buttons for Button Day. Give each child a few buttons to explore. Ask each youngster to choose one button from his collection and compare it to a friend's button, just as the boy and his grandmother do in the story. How are they alike? How are they different? Guide children to compare colors, shapes, sizes, materials, and number and types of holes on their buttons. Then ask them all to deposit their buttons in a round tin—just like the one in the story—to be used later during Button Day.

Transition Time:
Pick a Button

Here's a way to pick partners or groups that's "sew" perfect for Button Day—or any day! For picking partners, fill a container with pairs of buttons. Ask each child to choose a button and then find the classmate with the matching button. The two will become partners for the next activity. For picking groups, fill a container with buttons in the same number of colors as you wish to have groups. Have each child choose a button and then find his classmates who have the same color button. They will become a group for the next activity. Easy!

Circle Time:
Button Patterning

Buttons are perfect for patterning! To prepare for this activity, look through your supply of buttons for flat buttons appropriate for making patterns. Attach the hook side of a piece of self-adhesive Velcro® to the back of each button. You'll also need to prepare an old shirt or sweater. Remove the buttons from the garment; then sew on the loop side of pieces of Velcro in the buttons' places. Prior to your circle time, hide a button for each child. Then, during circle time, sing this song to send your little ones on a button hunt:

(sung to the tune of "Mary Had a Little Lamb")

Buttons hiding all around, all around, all around.
Go see if you can find one
And bring it back to me.

When everyone has located a button, direct the children's attention to the garment you've prepared. Begin a pattern with the Velcro buttons and ask student volunteers to bring up their buttons to continue it. When the garment has all its buttons again, remove them and start again with a different pattern.

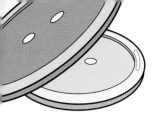

Project Time:
My Button Book

These books are cute as a button—and they'll help with sorting and counting skills, too! Each child will need 10 to 12 solid-colored buttons, a construction paper copy of the book cover on page 15, three copies of the text box on page 15, and three 5-inch construction paper circles. To make a book, a child cuts out her cover and text boxes. She glues one text box to the bottom of each of her three paper circles. Then she sorts her buttons into groups by color. She chooses three of her groups to feature in her book. Hot-glue one group of buttons to one of her pages. Then help her fill in the blank in the text box to correspond to the group of buttons. Assist her in completing her other two pages in a similar manner. If desired, hot-glue any leftover buttons to her book cover. Staple the pages together behind the cover and invite her to share her book with the class before taking it home.

Outdoor Time:
Button Relay

This relay race will challenge your students' coordination *and* their math skills! Divide your class into two teams, and have each team line up single file. Place a box full of buttons next to the child at the front of each line. Place an empty box for each team a distance away. To play, the first child in each line uses a spoon to scoop up some buttons, then walks quickly to the empty box and dumps them in. No picking up any dropped buttons! The student then returns to the front of her line and hands the spoon to the next child. Continue until all the children have had a turn. Then encourage each group to work together to count all the buttons they transported. Wow! That's a *bunch* of buttons!

Snacktime:
Cracker Coats

Mmmm…there are *edible* buttons on these cute coats! To make this snack, a child places a whole graham cracker and two graham cracker sections on a napkin as shown. She uses a plastic knife or a craft stick to spread peanut butter on the crackers. Then she adds M&Ms® candies to make buttons down the front of her cracker coat. Go ahead—bite into those buttons!

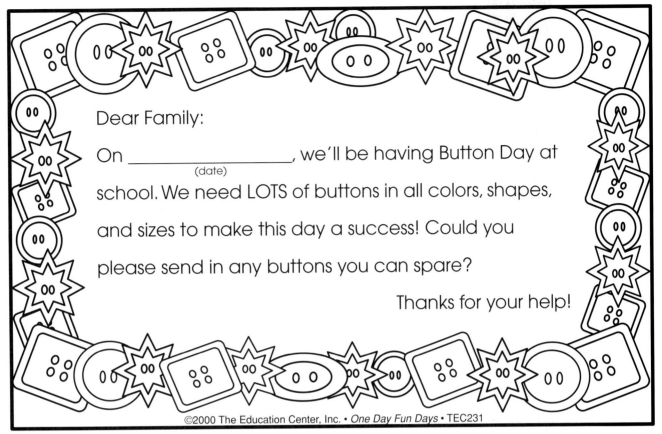

Dear Family:

On _____, we'll be having Button Day at
(date)

school. We need LOTS of buttons in all colors, shapes,

and sizes to make this day a success! Could you

please send in any buttons you can spare?

Thanks for your help!

©2000 The Education Center, Inc. • *One Day Fun Days* • TEC231

Book Cover and Text Box
Use with "My Button Book" on page 14.

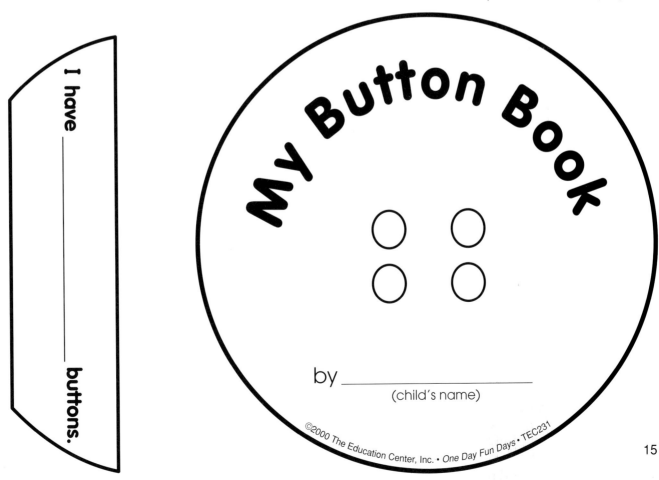

I have _____ buttons.

My Button Book

by _____
(child's name)

©2000 The Education Center, Inc. • *One Day Fun Days* • TEC231

15

COOKIE DAY

Crunch and munch your way through a single day of fun lessons about cookies, or use some of the ideas presented here to extend a unit on food, baking, or the letter *C*.

ideas contributed by Nancy M. Lotzer

CIRCLE TIME:
COUNTING COOKIES

Get parents involved in your Cookie Day by sending home copies of the note on page 18 a few days beforehand. On a sheet of chart paper, list all the types of cookies mentioned in the note. Display the chart in your group area.

As each child arrives on Cookie Day, help him make tally marks on the large chart to match his returned note. (Invite children who forgot their sheets or had no cookies at home to choose two or three favorite types of cookies and make tally marks beside those.) At circle time, discuss the results shown on the chart. Ask your group which cookie type appears to have the greatest number of tally marks. Which type seems to have the fewest? Then count the tally marks beside each type of cookie and write the numerals on the chart. Did youngsters assess the chart correctly?

> Cookies at Home
> 2 Animal Cookies //
> 3 Chocolate Chip Cookies ///
> 1 Sandwich Cookies /
> 1 Newton-Type Cookies /
> 2 Peanut Butter Cookies //
> 3 Sugar Cookies ///
> 1 Vanilla Wafers /
>   Others:
>   Pink Wafers
>   Gingersnaps

TRANSITION TIME:
THE COOKIE JAR

Here's a sweet way to choose partners or groups for Cookie Day. Make a class supply of the cookie patterns on page 18. Cut the cookies apart and place them all in a cookie jar. If you wish to have students pair up for an activity, have everyone draw a cookie from the jar and then find a classmate with a matching cookie. If you wish to form small groups, have everyone draw a cookie from the jar. Then have youngsters group themselves by type of cookie. Chocolate chippers to the block center!

STORYTIME:
THE GINGERBREAD MAN

After reading your favorite version of *The Gingerbread Man,* invite your little ones to chase down some runaway cookies of their own. To prepare, empty a package of small gingerbread man cookies into an airtight container. Write a note that congratulates your students on locating the cookies; then attach it to the container. Make six to eight copies of the clue sheet on page 18. Then program each one with a different clue (similar to the ones shown) about where little ones might look for the cookies. Attach the first clue to the empty package of cookies; then post the other clues in the correct locations on the playground to set up a cookie treasure hunt.

After sharing the story, tell little ones that you've brought in some gingerbread men for them to enjoy. Then bring out the empty package of cookies. "Oh, no—the cookies are gone! But here's a clue about where to find them. Let's go!"

> Run, run, as fast as you can!
> You can't catch me. I'm the Gingerbread Man!
> The _old man and woman_ saw me near _the slide_.

> Run, run, as fast as you can!
> You can't catch me. I'm the Gingerbread Man!
> The _____farmer_____ saw me near _the water fountain_.

CENTER TIME:
ROLL, ROLL, ROLL YOUR DOUGH

Prepare for some "scent-sational" fun at your play dough center by making three cookie-scented doughs. Mix up a batch of your favorite homemade play dough. Divide the batch of dough into thirds. Roll out one portion of the dough and sprinkle it with one tablespoon of cocoa powder. Knead the dough until it is evenly colored. Into the second portion of the dough, knead one teaspoon of ground ginger and one teaspoon of cinnamon. Add one teaspoon of vanilla extract to the final portion of the dough and knead. Place all three doughs in your play dough center, along with rolling pins and cookie cutters. Then set your little bakers to work!

PROJECT TIME:
A GIANT BATCH
OF CREATIVE COOKIES

This art project allows for plenty of individuality! Invite each child to make her own giant cookie by making the choices and following the steps below. When all the cookies are finished, display them on a bulletin board covered with foil.

1. Square or circle? *Choose a six-inch square or circle precut from white construction paper.*
2. Light brown or dark brown? *Choose from these two colors of paint (mixed three parts to one with white glue in separate shallow containers).*
3. Brush-painting or marble-painting? *Use a paintbrush to paint your cookie. Or place your cookie shape into a shallow box and then add a few marbles dipped into the paint color of your choice. Tilt the box to make the marbles roll over the cookie shape.*
4. Plain or chocolate chips? *Take a 3" x 4" piece of dark brown construction paper and cut out as many chocolate chips as you'd like to stick onto your cookie. Or don't add any at all!*

RHYTHM-AND-
RHYME TIME:
CHIP CHANT

Mix some math into your rhyme time with this tasty counting chant. To begin, give each child a five-inch circle cut from tan construction paper and ten chocolate chips. Explain that each child should count his chips onto his paper cookie as you slowly recite the chant together. When you get to the second verse, he may remove the chips one by one—right into his mouth!

One chip, two chips, three chips, four.
Five chips, six chips—let's count more!
Seven chips, eight chips, nine chips, ten.
Let's take them off as we count again!

Teacher: This time backwards!

Ten chips, nine chips, eight chips now.
Seven chips, six chips, five chips—wow!
Four chips, three chips, two chips, one.
Eat that up, and we're all done!

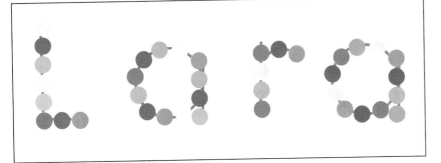

Project Time:
Dotted Names

Invite your youngsters to enjoy this reverse dot-to-dot project that will help with fine-motor control and name recognition. To prepare, gather a half sheet of white copy paper for each child, several ink pads in various colors, and an equal number of pencils with brand-new erasers. Lightly pencil a child's name onto each half sheet of paper. To make a dotted name, a child presses a pencil eraser onto an ink pad and then makes a dot print along one of the pencil lines in her name. She continues—using any colors she chooses—until she has dotted all the lines in all the letters of her name. Collect the finished names and bind them into a class book with the title "We Have 'Dots' of Friends at School!"

Storytime:
Ten Black Dots

You can count on dots to be lots of fun with a reading of Donald Crews's *Ten Black Dots* (Mulberry Books). After sharing this story, everyone will be seeing (and counting) dots *everywhere!* So head out on a dot hunt around your school or center. Here's a song for little ones to sing as they go dot-spotting:

(sung to the tune of "This Old Man")

Dots up high.
Dots down low.
Dots are everywhere we go!
So we're off to find dots.
How many will we see?
Let's all count them: one, two, three!

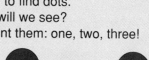

Center Time:
Dots by Design

Practice color matching, sorting, and patterning with this delightful dot center. In advance, gather a colorful supply of milk jug lids and make several copies of the dot board on page 21. Try one or more of these variations to tailor the center for the skill of your choice:

- Leave the dot boards uncolored and invite youngsters to make designs of their choice with the milk jug lids.
- Color the dots on the dot boards to correspond to your collection of milk jug lids. Have youngsters match the milk jug lids to the colored dots.
- Using colors that correspond to your milk jug lids, color the dots on each dot board to make a pattern. Leave the last dot uncolored on each one. Have youngsters match the lids to the colored dots and then continue the pattern by placing the appropriate lid on the uncolored dot.

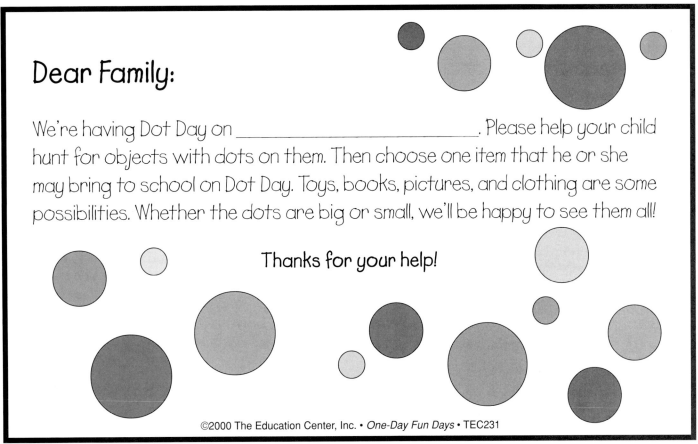

Dear Family:

We're having Dot Day on _____. Please help your child hunt for objects with dots on them. Then choose one item that he or she may bring to school on Dot Day. Toys, books, pictures, and clothing are some possibilities. Whether the dots are big or small, we'll be happy to see them all!

Thanks for your help!

©2000 The Education Center, Inc. • *One-Day Fun Days* • TEC231

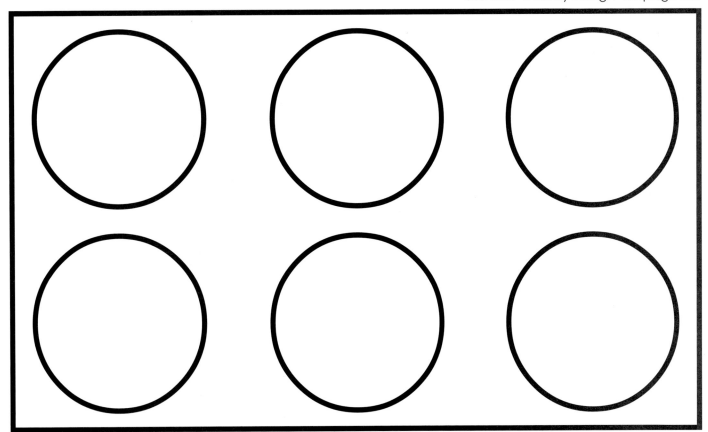

ELEPHANT DAY

Put on your safari hat and get ready to learn all about elephants! Plan one "elephant-astic" day or use some of these ideas as you study Africa, zoo animals, or the letter *E*.

ideas contributed by Kristin Ganoung

OUTDOOR TIME:
AN ELEPHANT AT SCHOOL?

Wouldn't it be fun to invite an elephant into your classroom? But there might be difficulties! Can your youngsters guess why? Lead your students in a discussion about an elephant's size. Share with them that an African elephant can be as tall as 13 feet at its shoulder. Then head outdoors with your young explorers to make a life-size illustration of an elephant.

First, help your students measure a piece of string 13 feet long. Lay the string on a sidewalk or blacktop area and help little ones use chalk to draw an elephant, using the string as a guide for the elephant's height. Next, measure another piece of string to match the height of your classroom doorway. Lay the string next to the elephant drawing and use it to help draw a door. Would an elephant fit through your classroom door? Your children will probably agree that the best place to visit an elephant would be in Africa—or at the zoo!

MOVEMENT TIME:
TRAIN THOSE ELEPHANTS!

Show the children some photos of elephants and discuss the sizes, shapes, and names of an elephant's body parts. Then ask your students to pretend to be elephants. How can they use their body parts to make an elephant's trunk? Ears? Tusks? Tail? Play a rousing game of The Elephant Trainer Says, played similarly to Simon Says. Give commands, such as "The elephant trainer says raise your trunk" or "The elephant trainer says flap your ears." If desired, give each of your youngsters a turn to be the trainer. The elephant trainer says, "This is fun!"

CENTER TIME:
WHICH ELEPHANT IS WHICH?

Scientists who study elephants in Africa become quite skilled at distinguishing among individual elephants. They look at the shapes of the elephants' tusks and the tattered edges and veins of the ears. Encourage your students to look at these and other characteristics as they sort elephant pictures at this center.

To prepare, make two tagboard copies of page 24. Laminate one copy. Cut the other copy apart on the bold lines to create cards. A child at this center "identifies" each elephant card by matching it to the same elephant on the laminated sheet. As a variation for this center, cut apart both copies of page 24 and have a pair or a small group of students use the cards to play a memory game.

PROJECT TIME:
ELEPHANT FAMILIES

Mix a little science and language together and you'll have a jumbo lesson on elephant families! Tell students that in the wild, an elephant family consists of many related female elephants and their calves. Some elephant researchers name the elephants in a family in a special way to help them tell the families apart. One family of elephants might all have names beginning with the letter *A* while another might all have names beginning with *B,* and so on.

Create your own elephant families by having each child draw an elephant on a sheet of paper. Have each youngster give her elephant a name. Help youngsters determine the families the class has created. Glue all the elephant drawings belonging to one letter family together on a sheet of poster board labeled with the family's letter. Encourage older students to help you put the families in alphabetical order. Then either display the posters around your room or create a giant class book, binding the posters together with metal rings.

SNACKTIME:
FEED THE ELEPHANTS

There's no better snack on Elephant Day than shelled peanuts or circus peanut candy! (Be sure to check for allergies before serving peanuts to your students.) Invite your students to eat their snacks as an elephant would! Explain that an elephant has one or two small fingerlike projections on the end of its trunk that allow it to pick up very small objects, such as peanuts. Have your little ones simulate this by using only their thumbs and index fingers to pick up their food. Then have them pretend their arms are their trunks and swing those peanuts right into their mouths!

STORYTIME:
SEVEN BLIND MICE

Share the story *Seven Blind Mice* by Ed Young (Philomel Books), the tale of some blind mice who come upon an elephant and try to describe it. Your students may think some of the mice's ideas are very funny, so try a little experiment with some "blind mice" in your own classroom. In advance, select several objects with distinct textures or shapes, such as a feather duster or a yo-yo. Keep the items out of sight. To begin, choose three student volunteers and blindfold them. Bring out the first object. Allow two of the volunteers to feel only *part* of the object. For example, one child might feel the feather duster's handle while the second child might touch only the feathers. Can either of them guess what the object is? Allow the third volunteer to feel the entire object before making a guess. After every child has had an opportunity to play a "blind mouse," discuss the moral of Young's story: "Knowing in part may make a fine tale, but wisdom comes from seeing the whole."

Game Cards

Use with "Which Elephant Is Which?" on page 22.

Feather Day

Youngsters will be tickled pink with this fine-feathered day of exploration! You might also add some of these activities to a unit on birds or use them to reinforce the letter *F.*

ideas contributed by Susan DeRiso

Circle Time:
Feather Facts

Begin your Feather Day with a reading of *Feathers for Lunch* by Lois Ehlert (Voyager Picture Books), the tale of a sneaky cat who tries to dine on 12 birds common to North American backyards. As the title indicates, he isn't very successful! Revisit the pictures of the different birds and talk about the colors and shapes of their feathers. If possible, show youngsters some real feathers in various colors and sizes. Then share these feather facts with your students.

- Birds have two basic types of feathers: *contour* and *down.* Contour feathers are the sturdy, sleek feathers that give the bird its shape. Down feathers are smaller and fluffier.
- Feathers enable a bird to fly and help it maintain its body temperature.
- Feathers give the bird its coloring, which can help it hide from enemies or attract a mate.
- Birds shed their feathers at least once a year. This is called *molting.*
- People use feathers as stuffing in pillows and furniture, as insulation in quilts and clothing, and as decoration on clothing.

Outdoor Time:
Feather Tag

Birds of a feather will *not* be flocking together when you play this creative game of tag. Start by taping a feather to the back of each child's shirt. Designate one child as the feather collector. Explain that it is his job to tag children and collect their feathers. Everyone else tries to avoid being tagged. Anyone who does get tagged gives up her feather and becomes a feather collector, too. The game ends when all the feathers have been collected.

Rhythm-and-Rhyme Time:
Ten Little Feathers

Gather a collection of colorful craft feathers to make the most of this tune (on right) that reinforces counting and color identification. To prepare, count out ten feathers in each color you wish to sing about. For each color, glue the feathers to a sentence strip and label the strip as shown. Hold up a strip and invite students to sing as a student volunteer points to each feather.

(sung to the tune of "Ten Little Indians")

One little, two little, three little feathers,
Four little, five little, six little feathers,
Seven little, eight little, nine little feathers,
Ten little [color] feathers!

1 2 3 4 5 6 7 8 9 10

Project Time:
Our Colorful Feather Book

This class book will create a lasting impression of your fun Feather Day! To prepare, duplicate page 27 for each child. Set out several paper plates with a different color of tempera paint on each one. Gather a number of sleek (contour) feathers to match the number of paint colors.

Have each child color her bird's beak and feet. Then have her press a feather into her chosen color of paint and then onto the bird outline to create imprints of the feather. Have her write or dictate the corresponding color word to fill in the blank. When all the pages are dry, cut them out and compile them into a class book. Add a white construction paper cover with the title "Our Colorful Feather Book." Record the poem on the cover as shown or on the first page. Finish the book by gluing colorful craft feathers to the cover.

Our Colorful Feather Book

Green feathers, brown feathers, black feathers, too.
Feathers come in many colors—even red, white, and blue!
Flip through the pages of our colorful book,
And you will see feathers wherever you look!

Yellow feathers

Center Time:
Clothespin Feathers to Count On

Youngsters' math and color-matching skills will increase at a fast clip with this center idea! Begin by duplicating the bird pattern on page 27 onto ten different colors of construction paper. Use a permanent marker to label each bird with a different numeral from 1 to 10; then cut the birds out and laminate them. For each bird, paint a matching set of clothespin feathers. Place all the clothespins in a basket, along with the birds. To use this center, a child clips the matching feathers onto each bird to make a corresponding set. What lovely tail feathers you have, Mr. Bird!

Snacktime:
Feather Cookies

These cookies are a "tweet" way to end your Feather Day! To begin, divide a roll of refrigerated sugar cookie dough into three parts. Knead a small amount of food coloring into each portion to make three different shades of dough. Roll out the dough. Ask a child to choose a color of dough and help him use a plastic knife to cut out a simple feather shape. Then direct him to use a plastic fork to make impressions down each side of his feather. Place a small strip of string licorice down the center of the feather to form its shaft. Bake all the cookies according to the package directions. Once the cookies have cooled, enhance the fork imprints by tracing over them with white decorator icing. (Use a tube with a very small tip.) Mmm! This feathery food is fantastic!

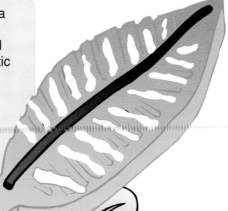

Booklet Page

Use with "Our Colorful Feather Book" and "Clothespin Feathers to Count On" on page 26.

feathers

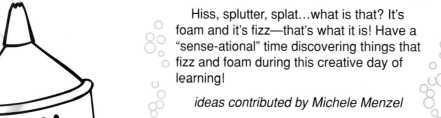

Fizzy, Foamy Day

Hiss, splutter, splat...what is that? It's foam and it's fizz—that's what it is! Have a "sense-ational" time discovering things that fizz and foam during this creative day of learning!

ideas contributed by Michele Menzel

Whipped Cream

COLA

Shaving

Circle Time:
Fizzy or Foamy?

Prior to your Fizzy, Foamy Day, send each child home with a copy of the note on page 30. When youngsters arrive with their items, talk about the terms *fizzy* and *foamy*. Explain that fizzy means something has air bubbles in it and you might hear it hiss or sputter, such as when you open a can or bottle of soda. Explain that foamy substances also have air in them, but they are smooth and fluffy like shaving cream or whipped cream in a can. Then invite each child to share the item she brought from home and have the class decide if it is something fizzy or something foamy. Form two groups based on this distinction. Did your class bring in more fizzy items or more foamy ones?

Rhythm-and-Rhyme Time:
A Fizzy, Foamy Chant

Review the items your little ones brought from home and make a list of them on your chalkboard or a sheet of chart paper. Then teach youngsters this chant, having them name a fizzy or foamy item from your list to fill in the blank. If they think of new fizzy or foamy items to chant about, add those to your list as well.

Fizz, fizz, hiss, hiss!
[Root beer] is fizzy, yes it is!

Foam, foam, feel the fluff!
[Shaving cream] is foamy stuff!

Center Time:
Fizzy, Foamy Exploratory

Caution: Young scientists at work in this center! Gather a variety of fizzy and foamy substances, such as carbonated water, Pop Rocks® candy, Alka-Seltzer® tablets, canned whipped cream, shaving cream, and meringue. Place the items in a sensory table or in a small wading pool. Duplicate the "Fizzy, Foamy Findings" record sheet on page 30. Put a supply of the record sheets at a nearby table. Encourage your young scientists to put on their lab coats (art smocks) and explore and discover all that hisses, sputters, froths, and lathers. Invite them to record their findings (with an adult's help) afterward. Provide supervision and remind youngsters to keep their hands away from their faces while at this center to avoid sore eyes and sick tummies.

Project Time:
Your Name in Foam

Here's a tactile treat with a result that's neat! To prepare this project for older children, write each child's name *backwards* on a separate sentence strip. Then spray some shaving cream onto a cookie sheet. Have a child smooth the shaving cream and then use his index finger to copy his backwards name into the cream. Lay a sheet of dark construction paper over his name and gently press down. Carefully lift the paper and observe—his name will be written correctly on the foamy imprint!

Invite younger children to make any design they wish in the shaving cream before making a print. Allow the foamy prints to dry overnight before displaying them or sending them home.

Outdoor Time:
Splat!

This movement activity is as fun and foamy as can be! To prepare, fill a few small wading pools or large tubs with shaving cream and various sizes of soft foam balls. Set up a painting easel near each tub and draw a target on it. (Or use sidewalk chalk to draw targets on a blacktop area.) Invite little ones to venture outside, wearing art smocks. Divide your class into as many groups as you have tubs and targets; then let the throwing begin! Encourage each child in a group to take a turn aiming balls at a target. When the fun's all done, have little ones toss the balls back into the tubs and use a hose to rinse everything clean.

Snacktime:
Fizzy, Foamy Floats

On Fizzy, Foamy Day, this frothy treat can't be beat! Give each child a plastic cup, a plastic spoon, and a drinking straw. Have her place one scoop of vanilla ice cream in her cup. Then pour in root beer soda until her cup is full. Ask her to listen for the hiss and fizz and watch for bubbles. As she sips, have her watch the float become foamy as the ice cream melts. It's fizzy *and* foamy *and* fun!

Dear Family:

We're going to have lots of fun on Fizzy, Foamy Day on

_____. You can help make this day extra special by
(date)

helping your child find a fizzy or foamy substance to bring to school.

Check your kitchen for fizzy things, such as carbonated water or

soda. Look in the bathroom for foamy things, such as

shaving cream or hair mousse. Anything that

fizzes or foams will do! Please place the item in

a bag with your child's name on it.

Thanks for your help!

Record Sheet
Use with "Fizzy, Foamy Exploratory" on page 28.

Fizzy, Foamy Findings

I liked _____ the best because

_____.

It looked _____.

It felt _____.

It sounded _____.

It smelled _____.

Scientist: _____

Flashlight Day

Rummage through the junk drawer and get out your flashlight. Then come along for this day full of "en-light-ening" activities!

ideas contributed by Susan DeRiso

Storytime:
The Little Book of Hand Shadows

Explore the magic of hand shadows when you show youngsters *The Little Book of Hand Shadows* by Phila H. Webb and Jane Corby (Running Press). Or you could share *Hand Shadows and More Hand Shadows* by Henry Bursill (Dover Publications). Either book will show little ones an interesting variety of characters they can make using only their hands and, of course, a trusty flashlight! After looking at the book, have youngsters pair up and take turns holding their flashlights and trying to create hand shadows. After they've had some time to experiment, invite each child to perform his hand shadow for the class. Your youngsters will be "de-light-ed" to show off this new skill!

Rhythm-and-Rhyme Time:
My Flashlight

Keep those flashlights out as you teach little ones this tune. Invite youngsters to flash their lights each time they sing "twinkle" and to shine the lights around the room when they sing "shining light on things for me."

(sung to the tune of "Twinkle, Twinkle, Little Star")

Twinkle, twinkle, my flashlight,
It helps brighten up the night!
When it's dark, it helps me see,
Shining light on things for me.
Twinkle, twinkle, my flashlight,
It helps brighten up the night!

Circle Time:
F Is for Flashlight

Here's a flashy way to reinforce the letter F. Prior to your Flashlight Day, photocopy a class supply of the parent note on page 33 and send a copy home with each child. Then collect a variety of objects, including some that start with the letter F—such as a feather, a flag, a toy frog or fish, a silk flower, and a football—and some that do not. During circle time on Flashlight Day, when your little ones have their flashlights in hand, dim the lights. Display one of the items you've gathered. Direct your students to turn on their flashlights and shine them on the item if it begins with an F but to leave their flashlights off if the item doesn't begin with F. After going through all the items, encourage little ones to think of other words that begin with F. If a student volunteers an appropriate word, he'll get a flashy reward!

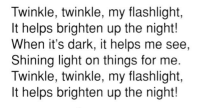

Center Time:
Shining Shapes

Put a few large flashlights to use as you reinforce shapes and fine-motor skills in this center. To prepare, make a copy of the four black shapes on page 33. Cut out the shapes and then tape each one over the bulb end of a separate large flashlight. Place the flashlights in an area of your classroom where you can dim the lights. Then place a pad of drawing paper on an easel in the area and provide some crayons.

Invite youngsters to visit this center in pairs. Have one child hold a flashlight no more than a foot from the pad of paper, shining a shape onto the top piece of paper. Have the other child use a crayon to trace around the shape. Then have her partner choose a different flashlight for her to trace, either on a clean section of the same paper or on a new sheet. Continue until she's traced all the shapes; then have the children switch places. When both children have traced all the shapes, invite them to color them in as they desire.

Project Time:
Flashlight Necklaces

Use this bright idea to make a lasting memory of your Flashlight Day. Collect a class supply of toilet paper tubes and three-ounce, unwaxed paper cups. To make a flashlight necklace, push the bottom of the paper cup into one end of the tube; then secure the seam with masking tape. Paint the outside of the resulting flashlight shape with black tempera paint and allow it to dry. Next, press a six-inch square of aluminum foil into the cup and fold the edges over the cup rim to hold it in place. Punch two holes in the open end of the tube. Then thread a 24-inch length of ribbon through the holes and tie the ends to create a necklace. Glue a copy of the flashlight phrase on page 33 onto one side of the tube. Have youngsters wear these necklaces home and share the details of Flashlight Day with their families and friends.

Snacktime:
"Flashcakes"

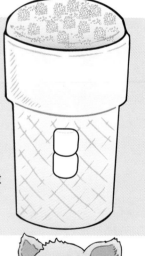

This glimmering treat will be fun to make and eat! In advance, partially fill a class supply of flat-bottomed ice-cream cones with prepared cake mix. Then bake the cones according to the box directions for baking cupcakes. Tint a container of white frosting with yellow food coloring. Then pour some sugar into a shallow bowl.

To make a flashcake, a child uses a craft stick to frost the top of her cake-in-a-cone and then dips the frosted cone into the bowl of sugar to add some glimmer. Next, she dabs a small amount of frosting on one side of the cone and sticks on two miniature marshmallows to resemble a flashlight's switch. Watch little ones' faces light up as they enjoy these creative snacks!

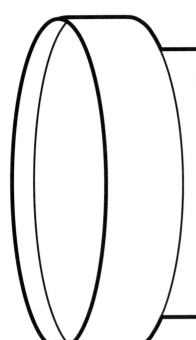

Hooray! We're having Flashlight Day!
We're planning some flashy fun on

_____
(date)

Please send your child to school that day
with a flashlight.

Thanks for your help!

Shapes
Use with "Shining Shapes" on page 32.

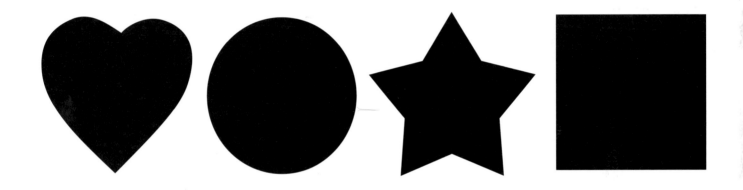

Flashlight Phrase
Use with "Flashlight Necklaces" on page 32.

Guinea Pig Day

There's just something about a small furry creature that piques the interest of youngsters. So use these ideas as an addition to a unit on pets or all by themselves for a cute and cuddly day of learning!

ideas contributed by Chrissy Yuhouse

Circle Time:
What Is It?

There's no better way to begin Guinea Pig Day than with the real thing. If you don't keep a guinea pig as a classroom pet, borrow one for the day from another teacher, a parent, or a local pet shop. But before you introduce your students to the furry visitor, send home the note on page 36. For each child, attach a copy of the note to a sheet of drawing paper. When students arrive on Guinea Pig Day with their drawings, ask the question, "What is a guinea pig?" Invite each child to share her drawing and her thoughts. Then bring in your guinea pig visitor. Allow plenty of time for observation and discussion. Older students may enjoy a factual book about guinea pigs, such as *I Love Guinea Pigs* by Dick King-Smith (Candlewick Press). Compare some of the children's drawings and explanations to the real guinea pig. Oh, so *that's* a guinea pig. Cute!

Payton

A guinea pig is a pig that is skinny.

Center Time:
A Home of Their Own

Re-create a guinea pig habitat with this fun idea for your sensory table. Fill the table with guinea pig bedding material, such as clean cedar chips. To make some inhabitants for this guinea pig place, fashion some simple guinea pig puppets from faux fur. For each puppet, use the pattern on page 36 as a guide to cut two pieces of faux fur. Use a hot-glue gun to attach the pieces along the inside edges. Cut ears and a nose from pink felt; then hot-glue them in place, along with two wiggle eyes. Place the puppets in the sensory table and let the imaginary play begin!

Rhythm-and-Rhyme Time:
The Guinea Pig Jig

After your class has met a real guinea pig, invite students to serenade your visitor with this tune!

(sung to the tune of "Head, Shoulders, Knees, and Toes")

A guinea pig has ears and feet, ears and feet.   *Touch body parts as they are sung.*

A guinea pig has ears and feet, ears and feet.   *Touch body parts as they are sung.*

And some whiskers and a nose,   *Gather fingers on either side of mouth; then pull away. Touch nose.*

But no tail on its seat, on its seat!   *Turn around and wiggle hips back and forth.*

Movement Time:
Guinea Pig Play Time

Guinea pigs love to crawl in and out or under and over almost anything! So invite your little ones to pretend to be guinea pigs as they negotiate a guinea pig playground in your classroom. Remove the end flaps of some cardboard boxes; then tape the boxes together to create tunnels. Arrange the tunnels between pillows or chairs low enough for youngsters to climb over and tables high enough for youngsters to crawl under. If you have standard indoor playground equipment, include that, too. Once the guinea pig playground is all set up, encourage your little ones to think like guinea pigs and get movin'!

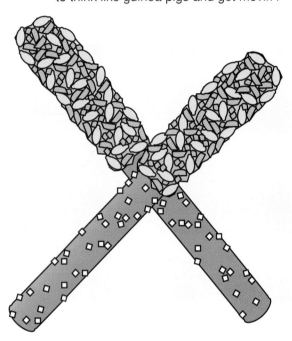

Snacktime:
Guinea Pig Grub

Like all rodents, guinea pigs have an interesting trait. Their teeth never stop growing! So they like to chew to help wear down their teeth. Guinea pigs enjoy crunchy foods, such as carrots or commercially made nut sticks, that give their teeth a workout. Invite your little ones to gnaw on these crunchy treats, just like the guinea pigs do!

To make one snack, a child spreads peanut butter around one-half of a pretzel rod. Then she rolls it in a mixture of crushed peanuts and shelled sunflower seeds until the peanut butter is coated. Let the crunching begin!

Storytime:
Guinea Pigs Don't Read Books

Share the wonderful picture book *Guinea Pigs Don't Read Books* by Colleen Stanley Bare (Puffin Books). Children will enjoy the humorous pictures showing things that guinea pigs can and can't do. After reading the book, label a sheet of chart paper as shown. Then have youngsters recall some of the activities that a guinea pig can and cannot do. Can they think of other activities to add to the lists? Maybe guinea pigs *can't* read books, but they *can* make great pets!

Can	Can't
make good friends	read books
climb	play checkers
squeak	tell time
	ride a bike

Parent Note
Use with "What Is It?" on page 34.

Dear Family:

On _____, we will be learning about a most unusual
(date)

creature—the guinea pig. Many children may not be familiar with this furry

animal, so we are posing the question, "What is a guinea pig?" Please ask

your child this question and record his response on the attached sheet of

paper. Then encourage your child to draw a picture of this animal. We will

all be sharing our ideas and drawings with the class.

Thanks for your help!

©2000 The Education Center, Inc. • *One Day Fun Days* • TEC231

Guinea Pig Puppet Pattern
Use with "A Home of Their Own" on page 34.

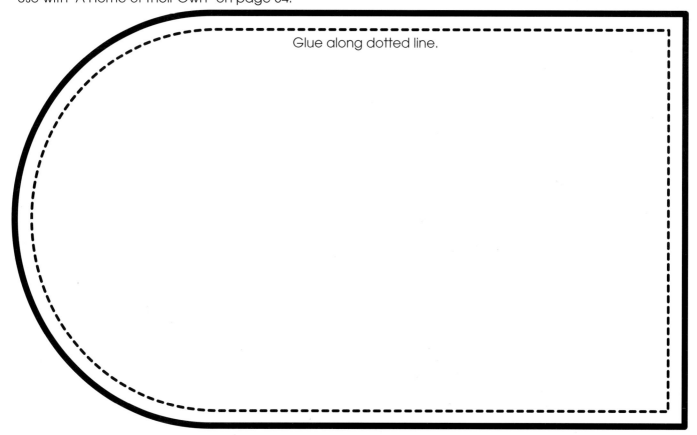

Glue along dotted line.

©2000 The Education Center, Inc. • *One Day Fun Days* • TEC231

Jiggly, Wiggly Day

Jiggly, wiggly gelatin is sure to make little ones giggle with delight on this special day!

ideas contributed by Susan DeRiso

Rhythm-and-Rhyme Time:
It's a Mystery!

Start the day by singing this song to introduce your little ones to the topic of jiggly, wiggly gelatin. Pause after each verse to see if they can guess what you are singing about.

(sung to the tune of "If You're Happy and You Know It")

It starts out as a powder in a box.
It starts out as a powder in a box.
You add some water that is hot;
Then you add some that is not.
It starts out as a powder in a box.

It comes in fruity flavors that you like.
It comes in fruity flavors that you like.
Your favorite might be cherry,
Or might even be strawberry.
It comes in fruity flavors that you like.

It jiggles and it wiggles in a bowl.
It jiggles and it wiggles in a bowl.
You eat it with a spoon,
In the evening or at noon.
It jiggles and it wiggles in a bowl.

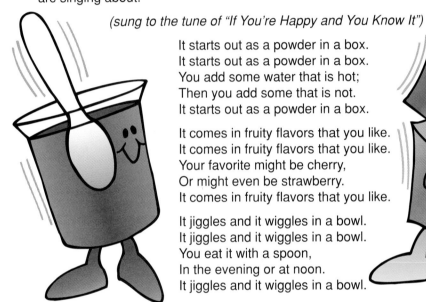

Storytime:
Shake My Sillies Out

Read or sing Raffi's *Shake My Sillies Out* (Crown Publishers, Inc.). Have youngsters revisit the illustrations and look at how the animals and people move in the story. Then ask a student volunteer to demonstrate how he would perform some of those moves if he were made of gelatin! Turn on Raffi's musical version of this song, available on his album *More Singable Songs* (Troubadour Records), and invite everyone to join in the fun! Remind youngsters to continue to be made of jiggly, wiggly gelatin as they clap, jump, and even yawn. Definitely silly!

Project Time:
"Sense-ational" Books

The fruity flavors of gelatin will have little ones' noses wiggling with delight when you make these scratch-and-sniff booklets. To prepare, make a copy of page 39 for each child. (Cut the treat poem from each copy and set it aside for later use with "Take Home a Treat" on page 38.) Next, fill a separate salt shaker with each of the following flavors of gelatin powder: strawberry, lemon, orange, and grape.

To make a booklet, a child first personalizes and colors her booklet cover. Then she colors the fruits shown on each page with the appropriate colors. Next she paints over each fruit with diluted glue and shakes on the corresponding flavor of gelatin. Once the pages have dried, she cuts them apart and staples them together to make a booklet. Encourage your students to take their booklets home to share with their families.

Outdoor Time:
A Jiggly Relay

This race will test your little ones' coordination as they jiggle and wiggle to the finish line! In advance, prepare several Jell-O® Jigglers® eggs. You can buy the molds to make these in your local grocery store or purchase them online at www.jello.com. Divide your class into two teams and provide each team with a spoon and a Jell-O Jigglers egg. Provide a turnaround point for the race, such as a traffic cone or a chair. Explain to students that they must carry the Jell-O egg on a spoon to the turnaround point and back and then pass the spoon off to the next child on their team—without dropping the egg, of course! Whether their team wins or loses, youngsters are sure to have a wiggly, giggly time!

Snacktime:
A Jell-O® Rainbow

Making this colorful treat is as much fun as eating it! Have students help you prepare it step-by-step as they make their way through Jiggly, Wiggly Day. You'll need a large glass bowl and five different flavors/colors of Jell-O® gelatin. Begin the day by mixing the first package according to the box directions. Pour it into the bowl and allow it to chill as you do the first activity of the day. (Follow the directions for the quick-set method found on the Jell-O box.) When you're ready for your next activity, prepare another box of Jell-O and pour it over the first. Then let that layer chill. Continue this process and you'll have a Jell-O rainbow by the end of the day. Scoop out individual servings into clear plastic cups and invite little ones to enjoy this perfect ending to a jiggly, wiggly day of fun!

Inside this bag is a magical treat,
Something that's really fun to eat!
Start with boiling water, ¼ cup.
Then sprinkle what's inside and stir it up.
Add ¼ cup cold water—but you're not done yet!
Chill it in the fridge until it's set.
What you will find is a fun surprise.
It'll jiggle and wiggle right before your eyes!

Jack

Center Time
Take Home a Treat

Extend the fun of Jiggly, Wiggly Day by setting up this center where youngsters can prepare a take-home treat. Make a class supply of the treat poem on page 39 and put the copies in a center. Also provide a class supply of small paper bags, crayons, glue, a tablespoon, a stapler, and a bowl of gelatin powder (each six-ounce box will be enough for eight treat bags).

At this center, a child uses crayons to write his name and decorate one side of a paper bag. He then glues the poem to the bag. Then he measures two tablespoons of gelatin powder into the bag before folding down the top and stapling it shut. What a fun reminder of a wonderful day!

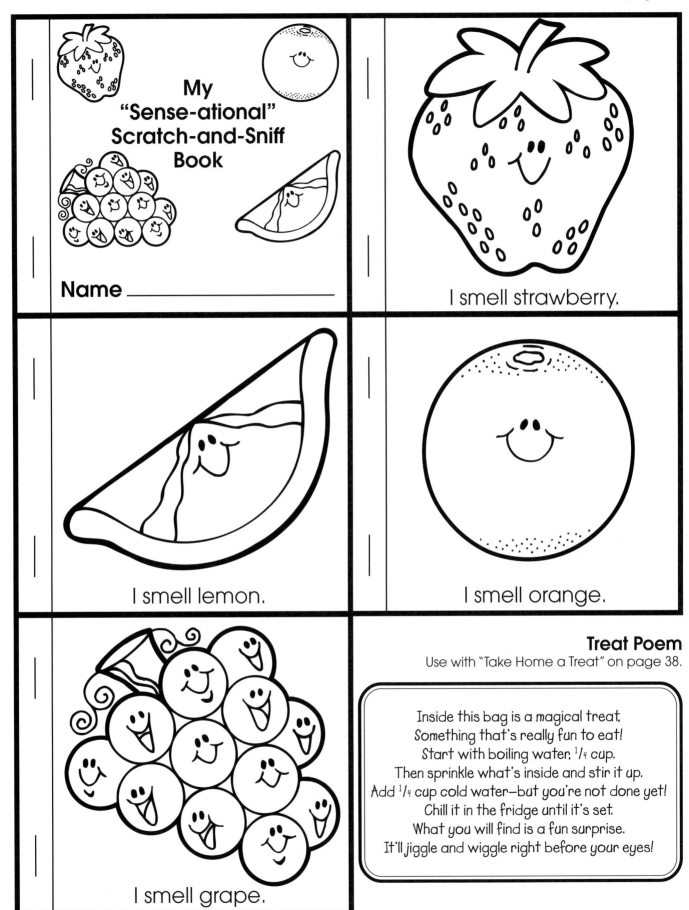

My
"Sense-ational"
Scratch-and-Sniff
Book

Name _____

I smell strawberry.

I smell lemon.

I smell orange.

I smell grape.

Treat Poem
Use with "Take Home a Treat" on page 38.

Inside this bag is a magical treat,
Something that's really fun to eat!
Start with boiling water, ¼ cup.
Then sprinkle what's inside and stir it up.
Add ¼ cup cold water—but you're not done yet!
Chill it in the fridge until it's set.
What you will find is a fun surprise.
It'll jiggle and wiggle right before your eyes!

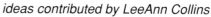

MACARONI DAY

It's a macaroni marathon! You'll need colored macaroni for some of the ideas in this unit. Follow the recipe on page 42 for coloring macaroni. If desired, duplicate the recipe and send it home to a few parent volunteers who are willing to prepare the macaroni for you.

ideas contributed by LeeAnn Collins

CIRCLE TIME:
CURVY OR STRAIGHT—MACARONI IS GREAT!

Invite little ones to compare two shapes of macaroni with this sorting and patterning activity. To prepare, duplicate the patterning card on page 42 onto tan construction paper, making one per child plus a few extras. Cut out each card, fold it along the dotted line so that the pictures are back to back, and then tape the sides of the card together. If desired, laminate all the folded cards for durability. Next, place a large sheet of bulletin board paper on the floor. At the start of circle time, open and dump out two boxes of macaroni—a box of elbow macaroni and a box of macaroni-and-cheese mix (the type that comes with a packet of powdered cheese). Invite each child to come up and take two different macaroni shapes. Ask little ones to describe their noodles. As they'll soon see, macaroni comes in both straight and curvy shapes.

Follow up this macaroni exploration with some patterning practice. Distribute the patterning cards. Use the extra cards to begin a macaroni pattern on the floor or chalkboard ledge, such as *straight, straight, curvy, straight, straight, curvy*. Have little ones come up one at a time to extend your pattern. Continue with other patterns as time and interest permit.

SNACKTIME:
MACARONI TO MUNCH

What's the perfect snack for Macaroni Day? Macaroni and cheese, of course! Cook some macaroni noodles, drain them, and keep them warm in a covered pot. Provide two or three types of cheese toppings, such as cheddar cheese soup, grated Parmesan cheese, and finely shredded mozzarella cheese. Serve each child a cupful of plain noodles and encourage him to try the cheese of his choice. Mmmm!

RHYTHM-AND-RHYME TIME:
MUSIC TO CLASSIFY BY

After circle time, invite youngsters to sort the real macaroni noodles into two groups by shape. Place two small pots in front of your group. Instruct the children to listen to the directions in the following song and then place the macaroni noodles in the correct pots.

(sung to the tune of "If You're Happy and You Know It")

[Macaroni with a curve] goes right here.   *Point to one pot.*
[Macaroni with a curve] goes right here.   *Point to same pot again.*
Get up and give a cheer
When you put a noodle here.   *Point again.*
[Macaroni with a curve] goes right here.   *Point again.*

Repeat the verse, substituting the phrase *macaroni that is straight* for the underlined words, and pointing to the other pot. Once you've identified the two pots, invite children to sing along as they sort.

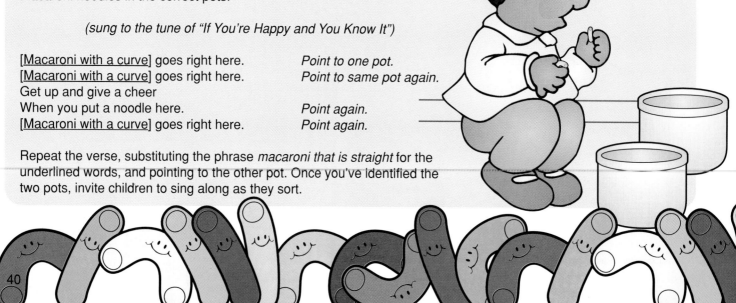

CENTER TIME:
MACARONI MUFFIN CUPS

Bring out the colored macaroni noodles for this center that combines fine-motor skills with more sorting practice. (See the recipe for coloring macaroni on page 42.) Place a bowl of colored macaroni in the center of a table and place empty mini muffin cups around it. Invite a child at this center to fill each muffin cup with one color of macaroni, using a pair of tweezers to pick up each individual noodle.

MOVEMENT TIME:
MACARONI IN THE POT

Have your group stand in a circle and act out this rhythmic chant.

Macaroni,	*Show one cupped hand.*
Macaroni,	*Show other cupped hand.*
Into the pot!	*Pretend to throw first one, then the other handful of macaroni into center of circle.*
I like macaroni!	*Nod head.*
I like it a lot!	*Rub tummy.*
Stir it up.	*Pretend to stir.*
Stir it up.	*Pretend to stir.*
Cook it up fine.	*Pretend to stir.*
I'll eat macaroni	*Point to self.*
Any old time!	*Open arms wide.*

PROJECT TIME:
MACARONI FACES

A little macaroni, a little glue...hey, that looks just like you! Youngsters will have a fine time creating these macaroni faces. To prepare, trace a five-inch circle onto a half sheet of skin-toned construction paper for each child. Provide colored macaroni and shallow dishes of glue. (See the recipe for coloring macaroni on page 42.) Instruct each of your young artists to dip macaroni noodles into glue and then press them on and around the circle to create a colorful macaroni face.

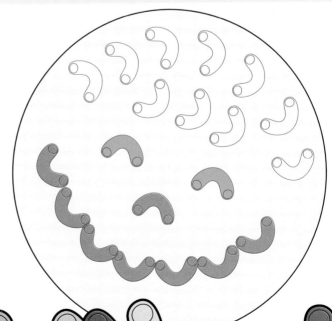

41

Colored Macaroni Recipe

Use with "Macaroni Muffin Cups" and "Macaroni Faces" on page 41.

Colored Macaroni

Pour three tablespoons of rubbing alcohol into a tightly lidded container. Add a few drops of food coloring in the desired shade. Partially fill the container with dried macaroni noodles and seal it shut. Shake the container until the macaroni is well coated. Scoop out the noodles and spread them out on two or three layers of newspaper to dry. Repeat, replenishing the rubbing alcohol and food coloring mixture as needed until you have the desired quantity of colored macaroni.

Macaroni Patterning Card

Use with "Curvy or Straight—Macaroni Is Great!" on page 40.

Pizza Day

Sink your teeth into this tasty collection of pizza ideas and get ready to gobble up the fun!

ideas contributed by LeeAnn Collins

Circle Time:
Which Topping Is Tops?

When it comes to pizza, everyone has a preference! Find out which toppings your class favors with this graphing activity. To prepare, photocopy one each of the pizza toppings on page 45 onto the appropriate colors of paper. Cut out the six toppings and glue each one to the center of a separate paper plate. Then display the plates on your chalkboard ledge. Give each youngster a spring-type clothespin. Have each student come up on her turn and clip her clothespin to the plate showing her favorite topping. Stop the voting periodically to discuss the interim results. Which topping has the most votes so far? Which has the fewest? Ask students to predict which topping will be the favorite. When everyone has voted, count the clothespins on each plate and discuss the results.

Storytime:
Pizza Pat

Pizza Pat by Rita Golden Gelman (Random House, Inc.) is a mouth-watering story, full of delicious pizza-building repetition. Your students will appreciate the predicament of Pat the pizza maker, who takes great care to prepare the perfect pizza, only to have some meddlesome mice snatch it up. After reading the story to your group, ask your students to list words that might explain how Pat feels at the beginning and at the end of the story. Discuss words—such as *happy, sad, proud, frustrated,* and *angry*—and have students recall points in the story when Pat might have experienced each of those feelings. Then invite students to create a new ending for the story. Reread the book with your students' ending. Maybe this time Pat will get to *eat* his perfect pizza!

Rhythm-and-Rhyme Time:
P·I·Z·Z·A

Follow up your topping vote with this catchy tune. Invite volunteers to supply the name of the topping in the second line.

(sung to the tune of "Bingo")

Upon my pizza, I like best
Lots and lots of [topping].
P-I-Z-Z-A
P-I-Z-Z-A
P-I-Z-Z-A
Pizza! I love pizza!

Center Time:
Pizzas to Go

This center takes a bit of effort, but it's made to order if you want your students to practice listening and following directions! To prepare it, photocopy several sets of the pizza toppings on page 45. Color the toppings, cut them apart, laminate them, and attach a small piece of magnetic tape to the back of each one. Purchase a round metal pizza pan, checking to be sure it's magnetic. Spray-paint the center of the pan red to resemble pizza sauce. Next, pop a blank tape into your classroom tape recorder. Record yourself ordering a pizza. For example, you might say, "I'd like a pizza with two pepperonis, one olive, and cheese." Ask other staff members to record their pizza orders, too. Then place all the materials, including the tape recorder and a set of headphones, in a center. Your shop is ready for business! Just watch as your little ones create special-order pizzas—and delight in hearing the familiar voices of their customers!

Snacktime:
Pizzas With a New Flavor

Invite your class to snack on some pizzas with a new flavor—fruit flavor! First mix up a batch of Fruity Pizza Spread following the recipe shown below. Then have each child use a craft stick to add some spread to one-half of an English muffin. Invite him to add the fruits of his choice from a selection of sliced fruits, such as apples, bananas, strawberries, and kiwi. These fruity pizzas are ready to eat—no baking required!

Fruity Pizza Spread
(makes enough for 15 pizzas)

Mix together one 8-ounce package of cream cheese (softened) with 1/3 cup sugar.

Movement Time:
Pat Some Pizzas

Give each child a golf-ball-sized scoop of uncolored play dough and encourage students to work those arm and hand muscles to the rhythm of this chant. By the end of the chant, the "pizza crusts" should be the right size. Then bring out various colors of play dough and have little ones add some colorful toppings to their play dough pizzas.

One pizza,
Two pizzas,
Three pizzas,
Four!
Flatten that dough just a little more.

Five pizzas,
Six pizzas,
Seven pizzas,
Eight!
Our little pizzas are gonna be great!

Nine pizzas,
Ten pizzas,
Yum! Yum! Yum!
Making yummy pizza is so much fun!

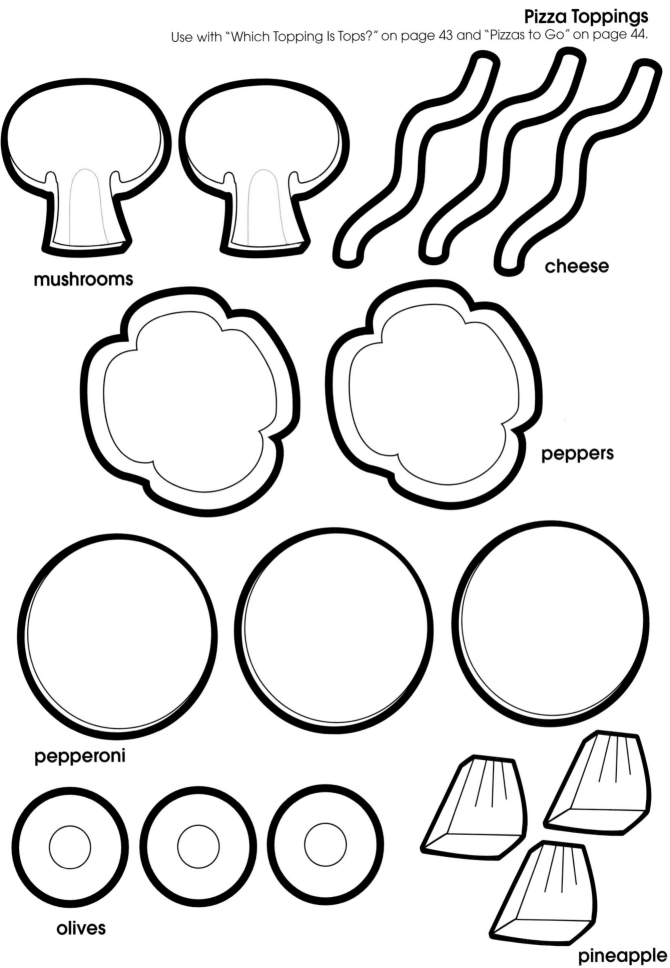

mushrooms

cheese

peppers

pepperoni

olives

pineapple

Ring-a-ling Day

Bells will be ringing in your classroom on this day devoted to bells and other things that ring.

ideas contributed by Susan DeRiso

Circle Time:
A Jingling Jamboree

Prior to your Ring-a-ling Day, send each child home with a copy of the note on page 48. During circle time on Ring-a-ling Day, invite each child to show and tell about the bell he brought—where did it come from? What does its ring sound like? Then group the bells by size. Determine which size bell you have the most and the fewest of—small, medium, or large. Then compare the different sounds the bells make. Which bells make the highest/ lowest sounds? The softest? The loudest? Then ring in the day with a jingling jamboree as students proudly ring their bells and march around your classroom.

Center Time:
Things That Ring

This sorting center sounds like fun! To prepare it, gather a variety of objects that ring, such as a toy telephone, a bicycle bell, a kitchen timer, a set of wind chimes, and a cowbell. Place these items in a center, along with some items that do *not* ring, such as a block, a toy truck, a doll, a yo-yo, and a book. Label a large box "Things That Ring" and place it in the center. Encourage each child who visits this area to sort through the items and place the things that ring in the box. If desired, make the center self-checking by taking a photo of the group of ringing things and gluing it to the bottom of the box.

Things That Ring

Rhythm-and-Rhyme Time:
Ring and Sing

Put the bells your youngsters brought from home to further use with this ring-along song. Direct your little ones to ring their bells as indicated by each verse.

(sung to the tune of "Row, Row, Row Your Boat")

Ring, ring, ring your bell,
As **softly** as can be.
Ring-a-ling, ting-a-ling,
It's fun for you and me!

Ring, ring, ring your bell,
As **loudly** as can be.
Ring-a-ling, ting-a-ling,
It's fun for you and me!

Ring, ring, ring your bell,
As **quickly** as can be.
Ring-a-ling, ting-a-ling,
It's fun for you and me!

Ring, ring, ring your bell,
As **slowly** as can be.
Ring-a-ling, ting-a-ling,
It's fun for you and me!

Project Time:
Glimmering Gifts

These beautiful bells are sure to become family favorites, since they're made by your students! To make one, paint the outside (including the bottom) of a paper cup with blue tempera paint. Add a sprinkle of gold glitter; then allow the cup to dry completely. Use a pencil to punch two holes through the cup bottom. Push one end of a 36-inch length of curling ribbon into one hole; then thread two jingle bells onto the ribbon and push the same end back through the other hole, so that the jingle bells are then inside the cup. Cut out a copy of the poem on page 48. Punch a hole as indicated; then thread the poem cutout onto one end of the ribbon. Tie the ribbon into a bow. Ring-a-ling! This gift is for you!

Wedding bells, doorbells, sleigh bells, too.
There are so many bells, yes, it's true.
But this little bell of gold and blue
Is special because I made it for you!

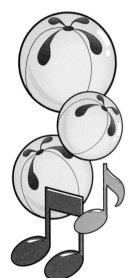

Movement Time:
Caught by the Bell

Play this bell-ringing version of "London Bridge" to get your youngsters up and moving! First, choose one child to be the bell ringer and give him a bell. Have two players form a bell shape (joining their hands to make an arch as they would for "London Bridge"). Have the remaining students line up and march one by one under the bell shape as the bell ringer plays his bell. At any given point, the bell ringer may stop ringing the bell and the two children will lower their arms and "catch" someone between them. The caught player sits out until another child is caught. Then the two form a second bell shape for the others to march under. Keep playing until all the children are part of a bell shape.

Storytime:
Telephone

In the silly story *Telephone* by Jamey Gambrell (North-South Books Inc.), a ringing telephone means callers with outrageous requests. From baboons who want spoons to doves demanding gloves, this rhyming tale will delight your young readers. Follow up the story with this version of the game Telephone. To play, you'll need a toy telephone, a small bell, and a favorite tongue twister. Seat youngsters in a circle and give the child next to you the phone. Ring the bell and have the child "answer" the phone. Whisper a tongue twister into her ear. Then have her hang up and pass the phone to the child next to her. Give her the bell and have her repeat the procedure—ringing the bell and whispering the message to her classmate when she answers the phone. Continue until everyone has heard the message and repeated it. Then share the original tongue twister and enjoy the laughter!

**Bells that jingle, bells of brass,
Bells will be ringing in our class!**

Dear Family:

On _____, we will be having
(date)
Ring-a-ling Day at school! Please have your child
bring a bell to school that day.

Thanks for your help!

Bell Poem
Use with "Glimmering Gifts" on page 47.

Wedding bells, doorbells, sleigh bells, too.
There are so many bells, yes, it's true.
But this little bell of gold and blue
Is special because I made it for you!

Wedding bells, doorbells, sleigh bells, too.
There are so many bells, yes, it's true.
But this little bell of gold and blue
Is special because I made it for you!

Slippery, Slimy Day

Your class will be oozing enthusiasm over this fun-filled day devoted to exploring the slippery, slimy side of learning! When the day is done, share the fun with parents by sending home copies of "The Ooze News" on page 51.

ideas contributed by Rhonda Dominguez and Lola M. Smith

Circle Time:
Let's Sing About Slime!

Welcome your little ones to this unusual day with this delightful ditty. Then follow up by asking them to help you list slippery and slimy things on your chalkboard or on a sheet of chart paper.

(sung to the tune of "It's Howdy Doody Time")

It's Slippery Slimy Day,
And we are going to play
With lots of icky goo,
And some that's sticky, too!

It's time to squash and squish
With all the ooze you wish!
Let's play with slime today
And watch time slip away!

Slippery, Slimy Stuff

soap	fish
bubbles	snails
slugs	ice
worms	mud

Outdoor Time:
Slippery Fish

This activity will have your young-sters grabbing and giggling! Prepare this outdoor center by partially blow-ing up several small, round balloons. Knot the balloons and use a perma-nent marker to draw eyes and fins on them so that they resemble fish. Place the balloon fish in a small wad-ing pool with just a bit of water and enough dish detergent to make them super slippery! Then invite your stu-dents to put on smocks and try their hands at catching these elusive fish. Whoops—another one got away!

Project Time:
Tasty Fingerpainting

This fun fingerpaint has a little something extra—it tastes great! Just mix a 14-ounce can of sweetened condensed milk with one tablespoon of cornstarch in a saucepan. Stir the mixture constantly over low heat until it begins to thicken. Remove it from the heat and add one teaspoon of green food coloring. Let the paint cool and refrigerate it until you're ready to use it. Invite your young artists to fingerpaint on cookie sheets or waxed paper. This fingerpaint is sure to turn any child into Vincent Van Goo!

Center Time:
Goop Soup

If your youngsters are hungry for a wild concoction at your discovery center, then Goop Soup is sure to hit the spot! Have each student who visits the center mix up a portion of Goop Soup by measuring five teaspoons of cornstarch and three teaspoons of water into a disposable bowl. If desired, provide food coloring to add to the mixture. Have him stir the mixture well before scooping, squeezing, and rolling it to his heart's content. Provide a few small objects and have him experiment to see if they float on top of the mixture or sink into it. When the fun is done, you can place the bowls outside and allow the water to evaporate. Then save the dried cornstarch for another day.

Note: This soup is for playing with, not eating!

Rhythm-and-Rhyme Time:
I'm Bringing Home a Slippery, Slimy Pet

Photocopy the patterns on page 51. Color the pictures and then use them on your flannelboard as you teach youngsters this song.

(sung to the tune of "I'm Bringing Home a Baby Bumblebee")

I'm bringing home a slippery, slimy worm.
Won't my mommy wiggle and squirm?
I'm bringing home a slippery, slimy worm.
Ooo-eee! It slimed me!

I'm bringing home a slippery, slimy slug.
Won't my mommy shiver and shrug?
I'm bringing home a slippery, slimy slug.
Ooo-eee! It slimed me!

I'm bringing home a slippery, slimy snail.
Won't my mommy's face go very pale?
I'm bringing home a slippery, slimy snail.
Ooo-eee! It slimed me!

I'm bringing home a slippery, slimy eel.
Won't my mommy scream and squeal?
I'm bringing home a slippery, slimy eel.
Ooo-eee! It slimed me!

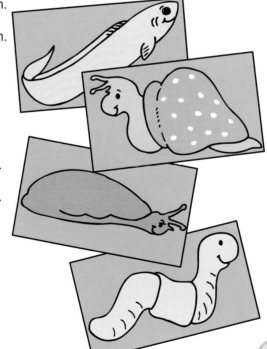

Snacktime:
Ooey Gooey

This yummy snack with an ooey-gooey center is perfect for Slippery, Slimy Day! To make one, a child first butters her hands. Then she flattens out an uncooked biscuit from a roll of refrigerated biscuits. She dips a large marshmallow into melted butter and then rolls it in a shallow dish of green decorator sugar. She places the coated marshmallow in the center of the flattened biscuit and then folds up two sides (like a burrito). She places the folded biscuit (fold down) on a greased baking sheet. Bake the snacks at 350° for about ten minutes or until lightly browned. When they are cool, dust them with powdered sugar and gobble 'em up!

The Ooze News

We had a great time at school today—it was *Slippery, Slimy Day!* Here
are some recipes we can try at home sometime. They're messy—but they're fun!

Tasty Fingerpaint

Mix a 14-ounce can of sweetened condensed milk with one tablespoon of cornstarch in a saucepan. Stir the mixture constantly over low heat until it begins to thicken. Remove from the heat and add one teaspoon of green food coloring. Let cool and refrigerate until ready to use.

Goop Soup

Mix together five teaspoons of cornstarch and three teaspoons of water. Add food coloring, if desired. NOTE: This soup is for playing with, not eating!

Ooey Gooey

1 uncooked refrigerated biscuit
1 large marshmallow
1 teaspoon melted butter

green decorator sugar
powdered sugar

Butter your hands. Flatten the biscuit. Dip the marshmallow into melted butter; then roll it in the green sugar. Place the coated marshmallow in the center of the flattened biscuit. Then fold up two sides of the biscuit (like a burrito). Place the folded biscuit (fold down) on a greased baking sheet. Bake at 350° for ten minutes or until lightly browned. Cool and dust with powdered sugar before eating.

©2000 The Education Center, Inc. • *One Day Fun Days* • TEC231

Flannelboard Patterns

Use with "I'm Bringing Home a Slippery, Slimy Pet" on page 50.

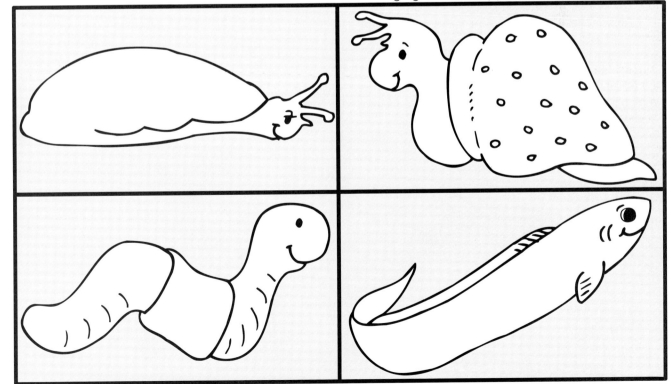

SPONGE DAY

Little ones will soak up the fun with these unique learning ideas! Before you begin, send home a copy of the note on page 54, asking parents for sponges in all shapes and sizes. Then you'll be set to spend a day spongin' around!

ideas contributed by Ada Goren and Kathy H. Lee

Circle Time:
Match the Sponges

You'll have all sorts of fun when you introduce youngsters to various types of sponges. In advance, gather a large car-washing sponge, a kitchen sponge, a shaped sponge for painting, and a bath mitt with a sponge side. Then make an enlarged copy of the patterns on page 54, color them, and cut them out. Back each cutout with a piece of magnetic tape and adhere it to your chalkboard or a magnetboard. Show little ones the sponges one at a time. Ask a student volunteer to match each sponge to its corresponding picture. In the shower or on the car—sponges are useful wherever they are!

Movement Time:
Sponge Toss

Combine math and motor skills with this game that's fun for indoors or out. To prepare, line up three buckets. Number the buckets with the numerals 1, 2, and 3. Adhere a tape line to the floor a short distance away. (Set a distance appropriate for your students' abilities.) Place a supply of small kitchen sponges nearby. Challenge each child to step up to the line and toss the corresponding number of sponges into each bucket. As a variation, take this game outside and partially fill the buckets with soapy water. What a splash!

Outdoor Time:
Sticky Sponges

After this activity, you'll never think of washing windows as boring again! Head outdoors with a can of shaving cream and some clean sponges. Spray some shaving cream on the outside of a window and then stick on a sponge. Wow! It stays—for a while anyway! After experimenting with this fun combination for a bit, provide a bucket of water and encourage little ones to use the sponges to wash away the shaving cream. It's good, clean fun!

Rhythm-and-Rhyme Time:
Sponges in Song

Squeeze the most out of this song—invite little ones to clean up your classroom as you sing it! Gather a small group around your water table filled with water and a mild soap. Give each child a sponge; then sing and encourage them to act out the words as they join in.

(sung to the tune of "Peanut Butter")

First you take your sponge and you
    soak it, you soak it.
You soak it, soak it, soak it!

Chorus:
Sponges gonna clean up!
Sponges!
Sponges gonna clean up!
Sponges!

Then you take your sponge and you
    squeeze it, you squeeze it.
You squeeze it, squeeze it, squeeze it!

Repeat chorus.

Then you find a table and you scrub it,
    you scrub it.
You scrub it, scrub it, scrub it!

Repeat chorus.

Then you take your sponge and you
    rinse it, you rinse it.
You rinse it, rinse it, rinse it!

Project Time:
Sponge Collage

When the sponge painting's through, what do you do? Put those stained sponges to good use with these unusual collages. Encourage youngsters to cut paint-stained sponges into different-sized pieces. Then have them glue the pieces to heavy paper or small boxes. It's squishy, it's colorful, and it's sponge art!

Snacktime:
Sponge Cake Delight

Sponge Day wouldn't be complete without this assemble-your-own snack! In advance, slice a sponge cake and thaw a carton of frozen strawberries. Drain the juice from the berries, and then place the berries and juice in separate bowls with small spoons. Give each child a disposable bowl. Invite him to spoon some juice into his bowl and then use a slice of cake to "sponge" it up. When the juice is absorbed by the cake, have the child top it with a spoonful of berries and a squirt of whipped cream from a can. Pass out the spoons and enjoy!

Parent Note

Dear Family:

On _____, we will be having Sponge Day at school.
(date)

We need some new, clean sponges to make this day a success.

We're looking for sponges in all shapes, sizes, and colors. Please send

in one or two by _____.
(date)

Thanks for your help!

Sorting Pictures
Use with "Sort the Sponges" on page 52.

Teeny, Tiny Day

These itsy-bitsy ideas will surely make for big fun in your classroom! Use this unit in its entirety or choose a few ideas to supplement an exploration of size.

ideas contributed by Chrissy Yuhouse

Circle Time:
Small Time Show-and-Tell

In advance of your Teeny, Tiny Day, duplicate the parent note on page 57 for each child. During circle time on Teeny, Tiny Day, invite each youngster to show and tell about her teeny, tiny treasure. Then challenge each child to complete a mini matchup—can she find a matching item of "normal" size in or around your classroom? Once everyone has matched her show-and-tell object to a real object that is at least similar, reward your little ones' efforts with a small surprise—a Hershey's® Assorted Miniatures® candy bar for each of them!

Project Time:
An Itsy-Bitsy Book

The itsy-bitsy spider crawled up the water-spout, but what would *you* do if you were very small? Have each child use his idea to contribute to this class book. In advance, make a class supply of the booklet page on page 57, as well as one copy of the booklet cover. Have each child illustrate his page by drawing himself doing something that only a teeny, tiny person could do. Write the child's completion of the sentence on the blank line. When all the pages are complete, staple them together behind the booklet cover. Conclude this activity by reading the book to your youngsters in a teeny, tiny voice.

If I were teeny, tiny, I could sit on a leaf _____.

Rhythm-and-Rhyme Time:
A Petite Poem

Continue the fun by reading aloud the following poem. Invite children to act out each line.

If you were teeny, tiny, you could ride an ant around.
And if it rained, you could hide beneath a mushroom on the ground.
A cotton ball could be your bed,
A marshmallow pillow for your head.
And you'd get full on crumbs of bread,
If you were teeny, tiny.

—Chrissy Yuhouse

55

Storytime:
The Teeny Tiny Woman

Now it's time for a teeny, tiny tale! Share Jane O'Connor's *The Teeny Tiny Woman* (Random House, Inc.). This version of the classic folktale about a teeny, tiny woman who finds a teeny, tiny bone—much to the chagrin of a teeny, tiny ghost—is perfect for very young readers. Follow up a reading of this story with a game of Who Took the Bone? Designate one child as the ghost. He sits in a chair with his back to the rest of the class. Place a teeny, tiny bone cut from construction paper beneath his chair. Then silently tap one child, who then takes the bone and returns to her seat. The children chant, "Teeny, tiny ghost, where's your teeny, tiny bone? Somebody took it from your teeny, tiny home!" The ghost then gets three chances to guess which child has the bone before you reveal the answer. The bone thief then becomes the ghost for the next round of play. No bones about it—this game will tickle your teeny, tiny tots!

Snacktime:
Teeny, Tiny Tasting Time

Fill your youngsters' little tummies with some tiny, tasty tidbits! Plan a micro menu for snacktime on this special day. Just think small—any miniature food will do! How about baby carrots? Cocktail wieners? Tea sandwiches? Mini pizzas? Serve it all on small paper plates and provide three-ounce paper cups for a sip or two of juice or water. These small snacks are sure to win big praises from your youngsters!

Movement Time:
Mini Movements

With this activity, your little ones will be on the move, but it may take a long time for them to get there! This adaptation of Mother, May I? will have your students listening, following directions, *and* working to control their bodies' movements. Play the role of Mother as children follow your lead. Call out some teeny, tiny movements, such as baby crawl, tiny twirl, bitsy bounce, teensy tiptoe, miniature march, petite prance, small slide, or wee wiggle. Inch by inch, little movements are a cinch!

Parents, We Need a Teeny, Tiny Favor!

On _____, we will be having Teeny, Tiny Day at school. In order to
(date)
have an assortment of teeny, tiny items to explore, we are requesting that
each child bring something tiny to school for show-and-tell. Specifically,
we'd like children to bring items that are miniatures, such as a toy car, a
piece of dollhouse furniture, or a tiny picture. So put on your thinking caps
and think small!

Thanks for your help!

If I were teeny, tiny, I could

_____ .

If We Were Teeny, Tiny

by _____'s Class

WORM DAY

Get ready to wiggle into some fun activities just perfect for a daylong exploration of worms. Or add a few of these ideas to a unit on gardening or the letter *W*.

ideas contributed by LeeAnn Collins

CIRCLE TIME:
FLANNELBOARD FUN

Count on this squirmy-wormy song and flannelboard activity to delight your whole group. In advance, cut an abstract piece of brown felt to represent a dirt pile. Then cut five worms from felt. Use the felt worms and dirt pile to illustrate the following song:

FIVE SQUIRMING WORMS

(sung to the tune of "99 Bottles of Pop on the Wall")

There were [five] squirming worms on the ground,
[Five] squirming worms.
One tunneled down, under the ground,
Leaving [four] squirming worms on the ground.

*Repeat, counting down until the last verse,
which should be sung as follows:*

There was one squirming worm on the ground,
One squirming worm.
He tunneled down, under the ground,
Leaving no more squirming worms on the ground.

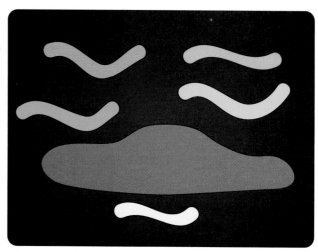

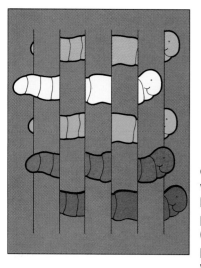

PROJECT TIME:
WIGGLE-WORM WEAVING

What do worms do best? Wiggle, of course! So invite your little ones to wiggle some worms through some brown paper "soil" with this weaving project. Copy the worm pattern on page 60 onto several colors of construction paper, so that you have four or five worms for each child to cut out. Provide each child with a sheet of 9" x 12" brown construction paper. Have each youngster fold the sheet in half (card-style) and then cut about six slits, beginning at the fold and stopping about one inch from the edge. (Precut the slits for younger children.) Have him unfold the paper; then demonstrate how to weave the paper worms over and under the paper slits.

CENTER TIME:
TUNNELS OF FUN

All your little ones will want to worm their way into your sensory center when you add these bags of "mud and worms." To make them, prepare a package of instant chocolate pudding as directed on the box, *except* substitute water for the milk in the recipe. Place about one-fourth cup of the pudding in a small zippered plastic bag; then add a four-inch piece of cooked spaghetti. Flatten the bag as you squeeze out any excess air and zip it closed. Add a strip of wide masking tape to further guard against leaks. Make several bags in a similar manner and place them in your sensory center. Invite a student to find the worm in a bag and then use her index finger to "draw" tunnels for the worm by running it across the outside of the bag.

STORYTIME:
INCH BY INCH

Enjoy the whimsical story *Inch by Inch* by Leo Lionni (Mulberry Books). Youngsters will be delighted by the clever inchworm who manages to avoid becoming a meal for an array of hungry birds. Review the long and short measuring adventures of the worm in the story; then get ready to do some measuring of your own in small groups. To prepare, duplicate the "Wormy Measuring Sheet" (page 60) for each small group. Also, precut several thick, fuzzy pipe cleaners to match the lengths of the worms on the measuring sheet. Give each group a sheet and some pipe cleaner worms. Have the children match the worms to the sheet and sort them by length. They'll soon see that worms come in all sizes. That's the long and short of it!

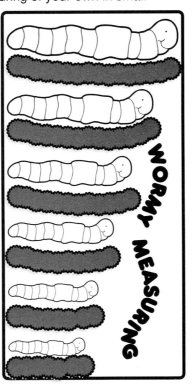

WORMY MEASURING

RHYTHM-AND-RHYME TIME:
WORMS DIG TUNNELS

Teach youngsters this lively tune and invite them to make up hand motions to go along with the words.

(sung to the tune of "Skip to My Lou")

Worms dig tunnels.
That we know!
Worms dig tunnels.
That we know!
Worms dig tunnels.
That we know!
Worms just love their tunnels!

(Shout) BUT!

When rain falls down,
Out worms go!
When rain falls down,
Out worms go!
When rain falls down,
Out worms go!
Worms don't like rain in their tunnels!

MOVEMENT TIME:
WIGGLIN' WORMS ON THE MOVE

Your little wigglers can expend some energy during a classroom Worm Crawl! Set up an obstacle course in an open area of your classroom or in a school gym. Make a tunnel by placing pairs of chairs about two feet apart (backs facing). Drape sheets over the chairs and—voila!—a tunnel. Inside the tunnel, set up some items for your crawlers to navigate over or around, such as a small pillow, large wooden blocks, or beanbags. Invite your worm wanna-bes to lie on their tummies and wiggle like worms through the tunnel. But watch out—there are obstacles ahead!

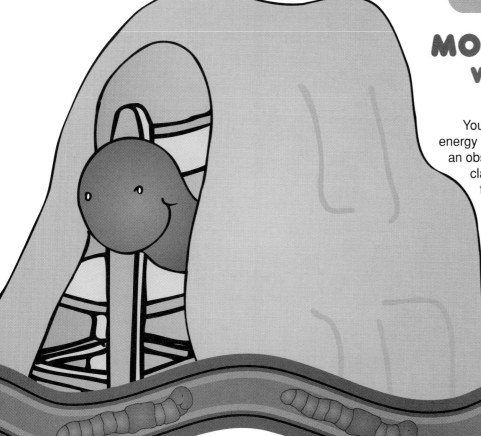

Wormy Measuring Sheet
Use with *Inch by Inch* on page 59.

Worm Pattern
Use with "Wiggle-Worm Weaving" on page 58.

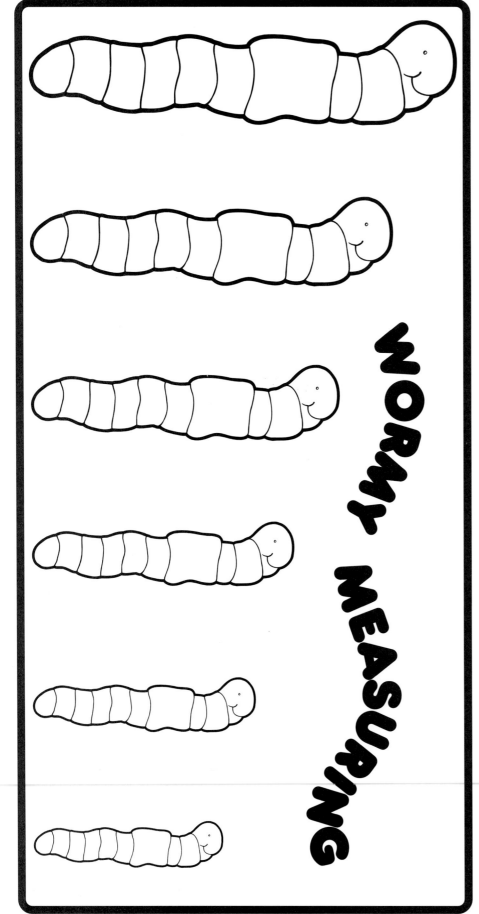

WORMY MEASURING

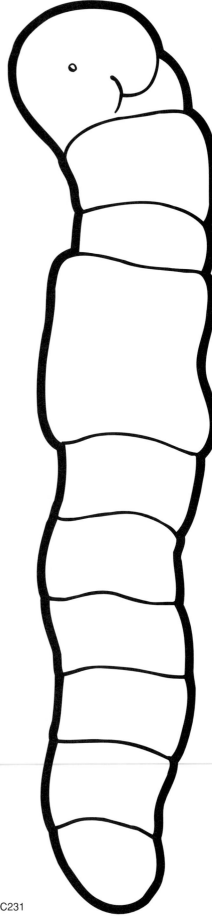

ZIPPER DAY

Zip-a-dee-doo-dah! Use these ideas for a one-day exploration, to supplement a unit on clothing, to practice self-help skills, or to reinforce the letter *Z*.

by Ada Goren

Circle Time:
Zippers Everywhere!

Prior to Zipper Day, make a class supply of the parent note on page 63. Send a copy home with each child in your class. When students arrive at school with their zippered clothing and items, conduct a sorting session. You might have youngsters sort themselves by where zippers are located on their clothing—shirts, pants, or jackets. Or place all the zippered items in a pile and have youngsters brainstorm ways to sort the items—by size, by type of item, by color of zipper, or by number of zippers on the item. Finally, ask little ones to put on their thinking caps and list any other zippered items they can think of. It's true—zippers *are* everywhere!

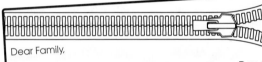

Dear Family,

On __Monday, October 5__, we'll be having Zipper Day at school! Please help your child choose at least one item of clothing with a zipper to wear to school. And please help your child locate another household item with a zipper to bring to school, too—perhaps a pillow, a pocketbook, or a travel bag. Can you find an unusual zippered item? We'll return all the items at the end of the day.

Thanks for your cooperation!
Mrs. Goren
(teacher's signature)

Rhythm-and-Rhyme Time:
A Zippy Tune

Follow up your circle-time sorting by teaching little ones this song. Invite them to zip the zippers on the items they wore or brought to school to provide the sound effects. "Zip-pee!"

(sung to the tune of "If You're Happy and You Know It")

If your [coat] has a zipper, zip it up!   *(zip, zip)*
If your [coat] has a zipper, zip it up!   *(zip, zip)*
If your [coat] has a zipper,
Bet you're feeling pretty chipper!
If your [coat] has a zipper, zip it up!   *(zip, zip)*

Repeat the verse as many times as desired, substituting the names of other zippered items—such as *pants, shirt, bookbag, purse,* or *pillow*—for the underlined word.

Center Time:
Zipper Practice

Zipper Day provides the perfect opportunity to have little ones practice their zipping skills. Gather a variety of zippered items, such as a jacket with a separating zipper, a sleeping bag, a zippered plastic bag, and some loose zippers straight from the fabric store. Place the items in a center, along with crayons and a class supply of the award on page 63. Invite each youngster who visits this center to work with each zippered item. Once he has successfully zipped each zipper, have him take an award, personalize it, and color it to take home.

Storytime: *Mrs. Toggle's Zipper*

Share the delightful story *Mrs. Toggle's Zipper* by Robin Pulver (Aladdin Paperbacks). Kindergartners will especially enjoy the humor of this story about a teacher stuck in her winter coat. After reading the story, ask youngsters to recall the various words used to describe the missing pull tab on Mrs. Toggle's zipper—*thingamajig, whatsit, doodad,* and *whatchamacallit.* Explain that people sometimes use these silly-sounding words when they can't recall the exact name for an item. Can your students list other words that fit this description? If necessary, help them out by providing words like *doohickey, gizmo,* and *thingamabob.* Then zip up this vocabulary lesson by inviting youngsters to vote on their favorite word from the list.

Zipper on the <u>suitcase</u>.

Our Zipper Book
by
Mrs. Carr's Class

Project Time: Our Zipper Book

Document the many uses of zippers with this class book. Purchase a box of quart-size Ziploc® Slide-Loc™ plastic storage bags. Program a sheet of paper with the words "Zipper on the _____." Make a class supply of this programmed page; then cut all the pages to fit inside the plastic bags. Distribute a page and a bag to each child. Then invite each youngster to look through magazines for a picture of a zippered item to cut out and glue on her page. Or have her draw her own illustration on her page. Write her dictation on the blank; then encourage her to slip her paper inside her bag and slide the zipper closed. (Make sure each child orients her page the same way.) Create a cover to slip inside a plastic bag; then stack all the bagged pages and staple them along the zippered sides.

Movement Time:
A Human Zipper

Just how does a zipper work? Help little ones better understand with a bit of observation and a movement activity. Begin by providing several zippers and magnifying glasses to your group. Allow some time for the children to examine the zippers closely and pull the tabs up and down. Then explain that a zipper works by connecting and disconnecting rows of metal or plastic teeth. Invite your students to simulate a zipper with this movement activity.

Divide your group into pairs. Have the children form two lines, pairs facing one another. Ask the children to stand with their hands at their sides. Then designate an extra child as the pull tab. (Or play this part yourself if there are no extra children.) Have the pull tab march through the open space between the lines of children. As she passes each pair of children, have them join hands. Once the pull tab has "zipped" the line, have her travel in the other direction, "unzipping" as she goes. Encourage the "teeth" in the zipper to provide some zippy sound effects. Be sure to give every child an opportunity to zip and unzip her classmates!

Parent Note

Use with "Zippers Everywhere!" on page 61.

Dear Family,

    On _____, we'll be having Zipper Day at
                          (date)
school! Please help your child choose at least one item of
clothing with a zipper to wear to school. And please help
your child locate another household item with a zipper to
bring to school, too—perhaps a pillow, a pocketbook, or
a travel bag. Can you find an unusual zippered item?
We'll return all the items at the end of the day.

Thanks for your cooperation!

_____
(teacher's signature)

Award

Use with "Zipper Practice" on page 61.

I can zip!

(name)

©2000 The Education Center, Inc.

Plan Your Own One Day Fun Day!

Topic: _____   Date: _____

Circle Time

Movement Time

CENTER TIME

Snacktime

Rhythm-and-Rhyme Time

Outdoor Time

Project Time

Transition Time

Storytime